I0814180

STORIES &
PUZZLES
for

courageous
GIRLS

STORIES & PUZZLES for COURAGEOUS GIRLS

World-Changing Stories & Word Searches from 24 Great Women of Faith!

ISBN 978-1-63609-832-6

Published by Barbour Publishing, Inc., 1810 Barbour Drive, Uhrichsville, Ohio 44683, www.barbourbooks.com

Our mission is to inspire the world with the life-changing message of the Bible.

Printed in China.

001963 0424 XY

HEY, GIRLS!

Here are 24 fantastic, fun word search puzzles for your enjoyment!

You'll read through the stories of courageous women of faith—including Esther, Hannah, Deborah, Lottie Moon, Amy Carmichael, Corrie ten Boom, Fannie Crosby, and more! As you read, watch for the **bold** words throughout each story. These are the words you'll search for in the puzzle grid. Of course, if you get stuck, answer pages are in the back of the book.

You'll be delighted and entertained as you solve these word search puzzles. . .and learn about extraordinary women who have made a difference in our world!

Amy Carmichael

AMY CARMICHAEL

SHE HAD HOPE

As a **missionary** in **India**, Amy Carmichael helped **orphans**—kids who had no **home** or **family**. She cared for more than fifty **children** who called her "Amma," which in their language means "mother." Being like a **mom** to all those kids was hard work, but **God** provided **Amy** with everything she needed. She made sure the kids knew about Jesus, and she taught them about God's **love.** Amy went about her work quietly, wanting nothing in return.

Maybe you know kids who need someone in their life like Amy. What can you do to help? Sometimes it's enough to just listen and be a good friend.

"I tell you, My Father in heaven does not want one of these little children to be lost."

MATTHEW 18:14

FIND THESE WORDS IN THE PUZZLE!

- ☐ MISSIONARY
- ☐ INDIA
- ☐ ORPHANS
- ☐ HOME
- ☐ FAMILY
- ☐ CHILDREN
- ☐ MOM
- ☐ GOD
- ☐ AMY
- ☐ LOVE

O	R	P	H	A	N	S	C	Y	F
N	M	Y	M	M	H	H	W	R	A
B	K	P	E	R	I	A	T	A	M
W	K	V	K	L	I	K	N	N	I
J	O	F	D	D	N	P	K	O	L
L	R	R	N	D	M	O	M	I	Y
R	E	I	H	X	O	V	Y	S	M
N	G	N	X	O	M	G	M	S	Y
N	H	X	K	B	M	V	A	I	L
B	J	T	Z	M	M	E	F	M	T

Mahalia Jackson

MAHALIA JACKSON

A PRAYER OF PROMISE

Whenever **Mahalia** Jackson sang, she **prayed** and promised God she would use her **voice** to honor Him. And she kept her **promise**.

Many people heard Mahalia sing, and she became **famous**. She recorded albums, sang for President John F. Kennedy, and, in the 1960s, was invited by Dr. Martin Luther King Jr. to **sing** at the March on Washington for civil **rights**. Using her voice to **honor** God led Mahalia to become an international **star**. Today she is remembered as one of the greatest **gospel** singers ever.

Have you made a promise to God? If so, ask Him to help you keep it.

My lips will shout for joy when I sing praise to you—I whom you have delivered.

PSALM 71:23 NIV

FIND THESE WORDS IN THE PUZZLE!

- ☐ MAHALIA
- ☐ PRAYED
- ☐ VOICE
- ☐ PROMISE
- ☐ FAMOUS
- ☐ SING
- ☐ RIGHTS
- ☐ HONOR
- ☐ STAR
- ☐ GOSPEL

G	R	S	T	H	G	I	R	Q	S
V	O	I	C	E	K	B	J	T	E
H	W	S	Z	K	D	M	A	C	S
O	B	N	P	E	A	R	C	U	I
N	M	C	Y	E	I	G	O	T	M
O	M	A	F	N	L	M	Z	B	O
R	R	D	N	N	A	S	T	Z	R
P	J	L	K	F	H	N	I	T	P
L	Q	N	M	X	A	M	F	N	T
D	T	X	M	Y	M	T	J	F	G

Deborah

DEBORAH

A THANK-YOU PRAYER TO GOD

Deborah was the only woman **judge** in the Bible. God spoke to Deborah, and she told others what He said.

She told a man named **Barak**, "An enemy general and his **army** are coming after God's people, and **God** wants them **stopped**." Barak asked Deborah to go with him to **fight** the army. Together they led God's army, the Israelites, to win.

Deborah **sang** a thank-you prayer to God. She **thanked** Him for allowing the Israelites to win the **battle** with their enemy.

Have you ever sung a prayer to God? Try it. He would love to hear your song.

"O give thanks to the Lord. Call upon His name.
Let the people know what He has done. Sing to Him.
Sing praises to Him. Tell of all His great works."

1 CHRONICLES 16:8–9

FIND THESE WORDS IN THE PUZZLE!

- ☐ DEBORAH
- ☐ JUDGE
- ☐ BARAK
- ☐ ARMY
- ☐ GOD
- ☐ STOPPED
- ☐ FIGHT
- ☐ SANG
- ☐ THANKED
- ☐ BATTLE

L F T C B A T T L E
H R W B A R A K Y S
A R R Q T G N C T D
R T H G I F T O L E
O Z G T R G P N Y K
B G A W P P N E H N
E O L R E N G A D A
D D K D M D K G S H
X J H L U Y T K K T
C K K J K F T K V L

Corrie ten Boom

CORRIE TEN BOOM

SHE TRUSTED

During World War II, German **soldiers** arrested **Jewish** people for no reason. They put them into **prison** camps where they suffered and **died.**

Corrie ten Boom was a **Christian** who trusted God. She and her family hid their Jewish **friends** inside a closet in their house, hoping that the soldiers wouldn't find them. But the soldiers found out! They **arrested** Corrie and her family and put them in a prison **camp.** Corrie almost died, but she stayed **strong** because God was with her.

When she got out of the prison camp, Corrie became famous. She traveled the world telling others how God had kept her safe during the scariest time of her life. You can trust that He will keep you safe too!

I will say to the Lord, "You are my safe and strong place, my God, in Whom I trust."

PSALM 91:2

FIND THESE WORDS IN THE PUZZLE!

- ☐ SOLDIERS
- ☐ JEWISH
- ☐ PRISON
- ☐ DIED
- ☐ CORRIE
- ☐ CHRISTIAN
- ☐ FRIENDS
- ☐ ARRESTED
- ☐ CAMP
- ☐ STRONG

A	P	R	I	S	O	N	R	M	W
R	N	N	M	P	M	A	C	L	G
R	S	A	J	W	B	P	J	N	F
E	R	I	P	D	T	L	O	R	H
S	E	T	M	X	I	R	I	S	C
T	I	S	T	M	T	E	I	X	O
E	D	I	C	S	N	W	D	K	R
D	L	R	Z	D	E	H	T	V	R
J	O	H	S	J	B	V	N	T	I
V	S	C	J	H	W	B	G	L	E

Harriet Tubman

HARRIET TUBMAN

SHE LED OTHERS TO FREEDOM

Harriet Tubman was an **African** American slave. After years of abuse from her master, she **escaped.** She traveled at night, following the North **Star**. With help from kind people, Harriet reached **freedom**. But that was not enough for her—she wanted to help **save** others. So she went back—again and again—finding ways to get her **family** members and other **slaves** to safety. Harriet **trusted** God while leading more than three hundred slaves to freedom.

Today Harriet Tubman is remembered for her bravery and faith. Can you think of a time when faith in **God** helped you to be brave?

You were chosen to be free.
Be careful that you do not please your old selves by sinning because you are free. Live this free life by loving and helping others.

GALATIANS 5:13

FIND THESE WORDS IN THE PUZZLE!

- ☐ HARRIET
- ☐ AFRICAN
- ☐ ESCAPED
- ☐ STAR
- ☐ FREEDOM
- ☐ SAVE
- ☐ FAMILY
- ☐ SLAVES
- ☐ TRUSTED
- ☐ GOD

B	T	Z	E	S	C	A	P	E	D
D	E	C	R	Q	K	N	P	L	F
E	I	T	G	Q	K	S	R	N	Y
T	R	Z	L	T	A	X	A	P	F
S	R	P	S	V	H	C	V	Z	R
U	A	J	E	E	I	P	X	L	E
R	H	C	S	R	V	D	R	R	E
T	M	K	F	T	O	A	T	W	D
R	D	A	M	G	A	M	L	P	O
Y	L	I	M	A	F	R	G	S	M

Catherine Booth

CATHERINE BOOTH

SHE SHARED JESUS' LOVE

In the 1800s when **Catherine** Booth was growing up, many people believed that **women** should not be **ministers**. But Catherine believed that God saw men and women as **equal**, one not better than the other. So she began to **preach**. Many people accepted **Jesus** as their Savior because Catherine was **brave** enough to share her faith with them.

Catherine and her **husband** created the Salvation **Army** to help others in need and lead them to Jesus. The Salvation Army still exists today and **serves** people in more than a hundred countries!

If Catherine Booth were here right now, she might say, "God wants everyone—men, women, boys, and girls—to do His work." He wants people just like you!

Peter said, "I can see, for sure, that God does not respect one person more than another."

ACTS 10:34

FIND THESE WORDS IN THE PUZZLE!

- ☐ CATHERINE
- ☐ WOMEN
- ☐ MINISTERS
- ☐ EQUAL
- ☐ PREACH
- ☐ JESUS
- ☐ BRAVE
- ☐ HUSBAND
- ☐ ARMY
- ☐ SERVES

W	E	N	S	V	Y	H	D	J	D
M	N	P	E	P	D	H	E	W	N
B	I	R	V	L	K	S	Z	E	W
H	R	E	R	K	U	T	M	B	H
U	E	A	E	S	M	O	V	L	C
S	H	C	S	Q	W	Y	D	R	L
B	T	H	X	W	U	R	M	Y	H
A	A	H	L	G	R	A	H	R	X
N	C	E	V	A	R	B	L	J	A
D	M	I	N	I	S	T	E	R	S

Hannah

HANNAH

AN UNSELFISH PRAYER

Hannah prayed asking God to give her a **baby**. She **promised** God if He gave her a **son**, she would allow the temple priests to raise him. He would grow up learning to **serve** his heavenly **Father**. God gave Hannah what she wanted, and Hannah kept her promise. She allowed the **priests** to raise her little boy.

Baby **Samuel** grew up to be a great man, a priest, a judge, and a **prophet**. He is remembered even today for his **wisdom**.

Hannah was willing to give God the one she loved most, her baby. Could you be that unselfish?

"You must give your whole heart to him and hold out your hands to him for help."

JOB 11:13 NCV

FIND THESE WORDS IN THE PUZZLE!

- ☐ HANNAH
- ☐ BABY
- ☐ PROMISED
- ☐ SON
- ☐ SERVE
- ☐ FATHER
- ☐ PRIESTS
- ☐ SAMUEL
- ☐ PROPHET
- ☐ WISDOM

X	R	P	R	O	M	I	S	E	D
L	S	T	S	E	I	R	P	X	R
M	E	V	W	H	M	C	D	Q	M
O	R	G	V	A	R	X	B	J	V
D	V	N	Y	N	C	F	F	K	S
S	E	Z	Y	N	R	A	N	D	A
I	O	B	M	A	T	B	G	Z	M
W	A	N	P	H	D	Y	J	K	U
B	R	P	E	V	N	Q	R	V	E
M	P	R	O	P	H	E	T	K	L

Pandita Ramabai

PANDITA RAMABAI

A PRAYER THAT LEADS TO GOOD THINGS

Pandita Ramabai grew up in **India**. Her family didn't know Jesus. They worshipped **false** gods.

One day, Pandita saw Christians **helping** others and sharing Jesus' **love**. This got her attention! Pandita wanted to know their **Jesus**, so she prayed and asked Him into her **heart**. She read the **Bible** and learned from Jesus how to help others.

Pandita set up **schools**, orphanages, and women's shelters. She **taught** others in India to live as Christians honoring the one, true God.

Do you believe there is only one true God? Pandita learned that trusting in Him leads to everything good.

"Have no gods other than Me."
EXODUS 20:3

FIND THESE WORDS IN THE PUZZLE!

- ☐ PANDITA
- ☐ INDIA
- ☐ FALSE
- ☐ HELPING
- ☐ LOVE
- ☐ JESUS
- ☐ HEART
- ☐ BIBLE
- ☐ SCHOOLS
- ☐ TAUGHT

A	Q	N	N	F	A	L	S	E	Y
T	K	C	S	C	H	O	O	L	S
I	J	D	R	E	K	L	G	O	Q
D	J	R	H	H	L	Y	M	V	T
N	T	R	A	E	H	B	B	E	H
A	Y	T	L	D	L	J	I	A	G
P	L	P	Y	K	E	P	I	B	U
N	Z	Q	F	S	W	D	I	T	A
V	Z	K	U	T	N	K	Z	N	T
Z	N	S	V	I	M	Q	F	X	G

Florence Nightingale

FLORENCE NIGHTINGALE

SHE WORKED TO MAKE THINGS BETTER

Even though her **parents** didn't agree, **Florence** Nightingale knew in her heart that God wanted her to become a **nurse**, so she went to nursing school. When **war** broke out in Britain in 1853, Florence and a team of nurses went to help British **soldiers** in military hospitals. The **hospitals** were very dirty. Bugs and rats were everywhere, and there wasn't enough **medicine** for everyone who needed it. Florence took charge and demanded that the place be **cleaned** up and more supplies brought in. She got busy **caring** for the men.

Florence continued fighting for clean hospitals and better patient care. It's because of her work that hospitals are clean and **safe** today. What can you learn from Florence's story?

All things should be done in the right way, one after the other.

1 Corinthians 14:40

FIND THESE WORDS IN THE PUZZLE!

- ☐ PARENTS
- ☐ FLORENCE
- ☐ NURSE
- ☐ WAR
- ☐ SOLDIERS
- ☐ HOSPITALS
- ☐ MEDICINE
- ☐ CLEANED
- ☐ CARING
- ☐ SAFE

H	O	S	P	I	T	A	L	S	C
D	R	N	U	R	S	E	F	A	S
M	S	Q	N	L	R	K	R	E	O
E	T	T	K	N	M	I	C	M	L
D	N	H	F	P	N	N	Y	R	D
I	E	X	Z	G	E	Y	C	C	I
C	R	R	W	R	Z	B	Z	R	E
I	A	K	O	A	M	L	K	G	R
N	P	L	J	R	R	E	F	A	S
E	F	C	L	E	A	N	E	D	F

Lottie Moon

LOTTIE MOON

A HEARTFELT PRAYER

Lottie Moon caused **trouble** at school. Her friends prayed and asked God to help Lottie **behave.** God answered their **prayers**. Lottie lay awake one night, thinking about her behavior. She knew she **needed** Jesus, so she prayed and asked Him into her **heart.**

Lottie's love for Jesus led her to **China** and missionary work there. She made lots of **friends.** Because of Lottie, many people **accepted** Jesus as their Savior.

None of what Lottie accomplished might have happened if her friends hadn't prayed. Do you know kids who cause trouble? Pray for them. You never know: God might have **plans** for them to do His work.

"But I tell you, love those who hate you. (Respect and give thanks for those who say bad things to you. Do good to those who hate you.) Pray for those who do bad things to you and who make it hard for you."

MATTHEW 5:44

FIND THESE WORDS IN THE PUZZLE!

- ☐ LOTTIE
- ☐ TROUBLE
- ☐ BEHAVE
- ☐ PRAYERS
- ☐ NEEDED
- ☐ HEART
- ☐ CHINA
- ☐ FRIENDS
- ☐ ACCEPTED
- ☐ PLANS

H	Y	A	N	I	H	C	G	H	K
B	B	E	H	A	V	E	K	P	L
F	R	I	E	N	D	S	E	R	A
Z	N	R	L	N	D	L	E	A	C
S	W	E	M	N	B	C	I	Y	C
Z	N	X	E	U	K	H	T	E	E
D	F	A	O	D	E	Z	T	R	P
B	K	R	L	A	E	Q	O	S	T
B	T	D	R	P	M	D	L	P	E
Y	N	T	L	M	F	N	M	L	D

Phillis Wheatley

PHILLIS WHEATLEY

A PRAYER OF TRUST

Phillis Wheatley was the first African American and the first US slave to **publish** a book of **poetry**. Many of her poems were about God.

As a **slave**, Phillis worked for the Wheatley family. They taught Phillis to read and **write**. She was **smart** and learned about many different things. Phillis especially loved writing! The Wheatley family **freed** Phillis from their ownership. As a free **woman**, she continued to write and sell her work.

The Wheatleys were **Christians**, and Phillis had learned from them about Jesus and prayer. She faced many problems in her life, but Phillis got through them all by praying and **trusting** God as her Helper.

Do you talk to God often? Do you trust Him as your Helper?

I have called to You, O God, for You will answer me.
Listen to me and hear my words.

Psalm 17:6

FIND THESE WORDS IN THE PUZZLE!

- ☐ PHILLIS
- ☐ PUBLISH
- ☐ POETRY
- ☐ SLAVE
- ☐ WRITE
- ☐ SMART
- ☐ FREED
- ☐ WOMAN
- ☐ CHRISTIANS
- ☐ TRUSTING

C	R	M	S	Z	T	J	N	C	X
W	R	N	G	L	K	Z	H	H	F
R	K	X	A	N	A	S	N	R	L
I	D	T	W	M	I	V	C	I	S
T	T	M	N	L	O	K	E	S	I
E	W	H	B	N	J	W	M	T	L
G	T	U	Q	K	X	A	X	I	L
R	P	O	E	T	R	Y	R	A	I
T	R	U	S	T	I	N	G	N	H
D	D	E	E	R	F	P	L	S	P

Esther

ESTHER

A PRAYER TO SAVE HER PEOPLE

Queen **Esther** had a big secret: Her husband, the king, didn't know she was **Jewish**.

An evil man named Haman **lied** about the Jews, and then the **king** ordered all Jewish people to be **killed**. Esther's cousin, **Mordecai**, heard the lies, and he told Esther. To **save** her people, Esther had to tell the king she was Jewish.

Esther **prayed** and asked God for **help**.

When Esther told the king her secret, he let all the Jewish people live. He rewarded Mordecai for being good, and he punished Haman for lying.

Esther knew to ask **God** for help. He is ready to help you too!

Do not worry. Learn to pray about everything.
Give thanks to God as you ask Him for what you need.

PHILIPPIANS 4:6

FIND THESE WORDS IN THE PUZZLE!

- ☐ ESTHER
- ☐ JEWISH
- ☐ LIED
- ☐ KING
- ☐ KILLED
- ☐ MORDECAI
- ☐ SAVE
- ☐ PRAYED
- ☐ HELP
- ☐ GOD

K	K	M	H	L	D	K	B	S	K
I	I	C	P	O	N	J	A	R	H
A	L	T	G	L	T	V	N	E	D
C	L	I	E	D	E	N	L	H	C
E	E	W	B	T	X	H	S	T	G
D	D	R	K	F	F	I	R	S	B
R	K	M	T	I	W	N	R	E	T
O	N	K	X	E	N	C	B	Q	N
M	X	M	J	V	Y	G	G	W	W
M	P	L	D	E	Y	A	R	P	D

Faye Edgerton

FAYE EDGERTON

A PRAYER FOR HELP

God created every **language** on earth. He understands everything people **say**. But with all those different languages, people don't always **understand** one another.

Faye Edgerton, an American missionary, wanted everyone to have a **Bible** they could understand. The **Navajo** people didn't have a Bible in their language. So Faye began the work of translating the New Testament into Navajo. She **asked** God for help learning the **words**. The Navajo language was very hard to **learn**. But Faye did it! She gave the Native American tribe their own Bible.

Maybe you would like to learn another language, so you can tell others about **Jesus** too!

There are many languages in the world. All of them have meaning to the people who understand them.

1 CORINTHIANS 14:10

FIND THESE WORDS IN THE PUZZLE!

- ☐ LANGUAGE
- ☐ SAY
- ☐ UNDERSTAND
- ☐ FAYE
- ☐ BIBLE
- ☐ NAVAJO
- ☐ ASKED
- ☐ WORDS
- ☐ LEARN
- ☐ JESUS

U	N	D	E	R	S	T	A	N	D
X	Z	H	Q	U	D	E	K	S	A
Q	N	F	S	R	Z	F	E	B	V
B	D	E	A	Y	L	N	G	W	R
I	J	S	A	Y	A	L	A	K	J
B	M	S	D	V	E	G	U	N	J
L	T	K	A	R	R	H	G	R	M
E	K	J	K	V	O	M	N	A	R
M	O	C	K	Y	G	W	A	E	B
P	B	M	V	R	V	G	L	L	M

Sojourner Truth

SOJOURNER TRUTH

SHE STOOD FOR TRUTH

Sojourner **Truth** was born a slave. After escaping to **freedom**, she became a traveling **preacher**, sharing truth from God's Word, the Bible. Sojourner knew there were good things worth **fighting** for in life. Her words and actions helped to free slaves and gain **equal** rights for **women.** Sojourner was never afraid to **stand** up and speak her mind if she thought it would help change things for the **better.**

Sojourner Truth is a wonderful **example** of someone who loved God and fought for everyone to be treated the same. She **trusted** that God would lead her through every situation.

If you stay close to God by praying and reading your Bible, He will lead you too!

"You will know the truth and the truth will make you free."

JOHN 8:32

FIND THESE WORDS IN THE PUZZLE!

- ☐ TRUTH
- ☐ FREEDOM
- ☐ PREACHER
- ☐ FIGHTING
- ☐ EQUAL
- ☐ WOMEN
- ☐ STAND
- ☐ BETTER
- ☐ EXAMPLE
- ☐ TRUSTED

E	D	E	T	S	U	R	T	M	W
Q	W	H	D	P	D	Z	O	O	T
U	F	M	Y	C	B	D	M	K	Q
A	B	I	R	V	E	E	B	H	E
L	N	K	G	E	N	N	G	T	L
R	T	Y	R	H	T	T	K	U	P
R	J	F	Y	F	T	T	J	R	M
D	N	A	T	S	Q	I	E	T	A
L	P	K	X	G	R	Z	N	B	X
P	R	E	A	C	H	E	R	G	E

Elizabeth Fry

ELIZABETH FRY

A PRAYER TO HELP OTHERS

Elizabeth Fry spent her whole life helping the **poor**. She saw terrible conditions in England's **prisons**, and she became like an **angel** to the women there. She prayed for them and **taught** them about God. Elizabeth asked the **queen** and other leaders for help making the prisons **better**. Her prison **mission** grew and was well known all over Europe. Many people were **helped** by Elizabeth's kindness. She never gave up. She **prayed** hard, stood up to those who were against her, and she made sure things got done.

How can you be like Elizabeth and help others? Ask God to show you what you can do.

The Spirit of the Lord God is on me, because the Lord has chosen me to bring good news to poor people. He has sent me to heal those with a sad heart.

ISAIAH 61:1

FIND THESE WORDS IN THE PUZZLE!

- ☐ ELIZABETH
- ☐ POOR
- ☐ PRISONS
- ☐ ANGEL
- ☐ TAUGHT
- ☐ QUEEN
- ☐ BETTER
- ☐ MISSION
- ☐ HELPED
- ☐ PRAYED

A	K	P	R	I	S	O	N	S	P
Y	N	O	H	K	R	H	P	G	R
P	O	G	B	N	X	T	N	K	G
P	R	T	E	R	G	E	H	D	N
K	R	A	F	L	E	B	E	N	O
F	L	U	Y	U	K	A	L	K	I
N	H	G	Q	E	N	Z	P	T	S
N	R	H	K	B	D	I	E	H	S
B	E	T	T	E	R	L	D	X	I
P	D	L	X	X	V	E	G	X	M

Clara Barton

CLARA BARTON

SHE MADE A DIFFERENCE

Clara Barton was very **shy**, but God helped her become **brave** so she could help others. In the 1800s during the Civil War, Clara helped **nurse** soldiers who were hurt. After the war was over, Clara worked to find missing soldiers and return them to their **families**. In 1861, she formed a group to help people called the American Red **Cross**. Even today, the Red Cross shows up when big **trouble** strikes—like fires, floods, and **storms**.

Are you a bit shy like Clara? Ask God to lead you. He'll give you the **courage** to make a difference doing **good** things in your community.

For God did not give us a spirit of fear. He gave us a spirit of power and of love and of a good mind.

2 TIMOTHY 1:7

FIND THESE WORDS IN THE PUZZLE!

- ☐ CLARA
- ☐ SHY
- ☐ BRAVE
- ☐ NURSE
- ☐ FAMILIES
- ☐ CROSS
- ☐ TROUBLE
- ☐ STORMS
- ☐ COURAGE
- ☐ GOOD

N	F	N	B	N	N	J	F	L	J
K	C	K	U	D	K	C	A	F	D
J	X	F	C	R	R	Y	M	A	E
T	L	Z	Y	O	S	H	I	R	G
K	N	Y	S	D	J	E	L	A	A
M	H	S	O	M	M	F	I	L	R
S	K	O	K	H	R	T	E	C	U
K	G	Z	J	F	T	O	S	T	O
E	L	B	U	O	R	T	T	H	C
B	R	A	V	E	T	Q	Q	S	Z

Edith Schaeffer

EDITH SCHAEFFER

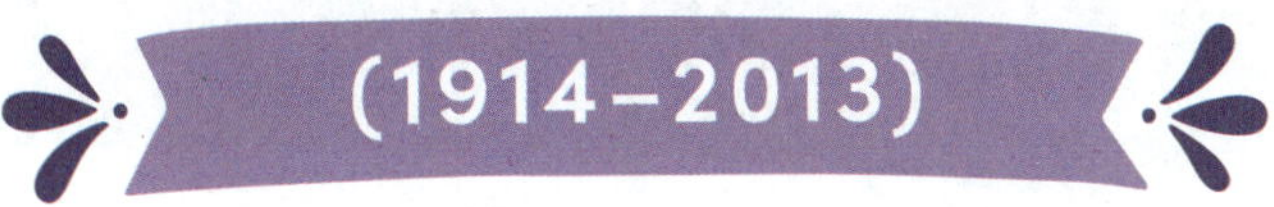

SHE WAS KIND

Edith Schaeffer and her family were missionaries who lived in a village in the **Swiss** mountains. They opened their **home** to anyone who wanted to learn about Jesus. Edith prayed, asking God to send those who needed to **know** Him. People began hearing about the Schaeffers, and they came to stay as **guests** in their house.

Edith never judged those who came. She never turned anyone away—*all* were **welcome** in her home. She cooked, cleaned, and **shared** with her guests about how much **Jesus** loves them. Her story is a great example of **Christian** hospitality—welcoming, warm, and kind—just like Jesus is!

What are some good ways your family can welcome **visitors**?

Do not forget to be kind to strangers and let them stay in your home. Some people have had angels in their homes without knowing it.

HEBREWS 13:2

FIND THESE WORDS IN THE PUZZLE!

- ☐ EDITH
- ☐ SWISS
- ☐ HOME
- ☐ KNOW
- ☐ GUESTS
- ☐ WELCOME
- ☐ SHARED
- ☐ JESUS
- ☐ CHRISTIAN
- ☐ VISITORS

J	E	S	U	S	M	C	S	Q	C
N	R	L	M	Y	D	S	Z	H	G
V	H	O	M	E	I	N	R	P	E
B	J	J	R	W	L	I	T	G	M
W	K	A	S	H	S	D	T	U	O
M	H	Y	M	T	L	R	X	E	C
S	F	T	I	I	K	C	B	S	L
B	G	A	N	D	G	N	H	T	E
M	N	L	J	E	L	X	O	S	W
S	R	O	T	I	S	I	V	W	J

Esther Ibanga

ESTHER IBANGA

A PRAYER FOR PEACE

In **Nigeria**, where **Esther** Ibanga is a pastor, Christians and **Muslims** don't get along. But Esther wanted to create a good **change**. So she reached out to Muslim women, hoping that together they might find a solution and maybe even **friendship**. She and her new friends began the **Women** Without Walls Initiative. Their goal is to reach Nigeria's **children** and help them get along, so someday there might be **peace**.

Esther was raised in a family that **prayed**. She prays every day for peace among **Christians**, Muslims, and people all over the world.

Do you pray for peace in the world? Think of three things you can do to help people get along.

"Do not hurt someone who has hurt you. Do not keep on hating the sons of your people, but love your neighbor as yourself."

LEVITICUS 19:18

FIND THESE WORDS IN THE PUZZLE!

- ☐ NIGERIA
- ☐ ESTHER
- ☐ MUSLIMS
- ☐ CHANGE
- ☐ FRIENDSHIP
- ☐ WOMEN
- ☐ CHILDREN
- ☐ PEACE
- ☐ PRAYED
- ☐ CHRISTIANS

G	M	U	S	L	I	M	S	F	C
T	C	M	H	P	N	V	A	R	H
N	M	H	B	M	T	J	I	I	R
E	D	W	A	M	X	R	R	E	I
R	N	E	Q	N	E	H	E	N	S
D	T	L	Y	H	G	W	G	D	T
L	D	F	T	A	O	E	I	S	I
I	N	S	H	M	R	N	N	H	A
H	E	T	E	T	N	P	K	I	N
C	J	N	L	E	C	A	E	P	S

Mary Slessor

MARY SLESSOR

SHE WAS MERCIFUL

Mary Slessor was a missionary in **Africa**. She was super courageous. She went deep into the places where African **tribes** lived. Few missionaries were **brave** enough to go where Mary went.

Mary knew that to help the tribes, she needed to live among them and learn their **language**. So that's what she did. The tribes learned not only to **accept** Mary but also to respect and **love** her. She taught them about **Jesus**. And even when they were not so nice, Mary was **merciful**—kind and caring—to them.

Did you know that God is merciful to you? He always **forgives** when you mess up. *Nothing* will stop Him from loving you.

For You are good and ready to forgive, O Lord.
You are rich in loving-kindness to all who call to You.

PSALM 86:5

FIND THESE WORDS IN THE PUZZLE!

- ☐ MARY
- ☐ AFRICA
- ☐ TRIBES
- ☐ BRAVE
- ☐ LANGUAGE
- ☐ ACCEPT
- ☐ LOVE
- ☐ JESUS
- ☐ MERCIFUL
- ☐ FORGIVES

L	L	J	B	H	E	V	O	L	R
U	A	F	O	R	G	I	V	E	S
F	N	J	M	L	A	K	T	A	Q
I	G	T	R	R	L	V	C	Z	A
C	U	D	S	N	X	C	E	C	X
R	A	Y	H	U	E	Z	I	X	J
E	G	R	J	P	S	R	T	L	Z
M	E	A	T	P	F	E	R	H	R
X	K	M	V	A	Z	N	J	L	G
T	R	I	B	E	S	G	X	R	T

Anne Hutchinson

ANNE HUTCHINSON

A COURAGEOUS PRAYER

Anne Hutchinson was one of the first **American** women to speak up about her **faith**. She lived in the Massachusetts Bay **Colony** when women were not allowed to **speak** up or lead others in prayer. But Anne, who thought for herself, decided she wasn't going to keep **quiet**! She held **prayer** meetings in her home and was arrested for breaking the **law**. Still, she stood up for what she believed was **right**. She bravely prayed in public and shared her faith with others.

Anne's actions helped give women the **courage** to continue speaking up and fighting for what they believe. Ask God to help you be courageous in your faith too!

Open your mouth for those who cannot speak,
and for the rights of those who are left without help.

PROVERBS 31:8

FIND THESE WORDS IN THE PUZZLE!

- ☐ ANNE
- ☐ AMERICAN
- ☐ FAITH
- ☐ COLONY
- ☐ SPEAK
- ☐ QUIET
- ☐ PRAYER
- ☐ LAW
- ☐ RIGHT
- ☐ COURAGE

G	N	W	W	K	T	Z	Q	D	V
B	F	A	I	T	H	U	H	N	E
T	S	J	N	C	I	C	N	R	N
H	P	K	X	E	O	A	B	N	N
G	E	V	T	U	C	L	X	R	A
I	A	B	R	I	P	L	O	R	R
R	K	A	R	W	M	D	W	N	T
G	G	E	Z	T	R	K	Q	A	Y
E	M	Y	V	R	V	M	R	P	L
A	F	R	E	Y	A	R	P	K	R

Mother Teresa

MOTHER TERESA

SHE SERVED OTHERS

Mother **Teresa**, a Catholic nun, traveled to **India** to help the **poor** people there. She nursed the sick, fed the **hungry**, and brought love to those who felt **lonely** and forgotten. Many people admired her work and came to India to help. As more came to **volunteer**, the group became known as the Missionaries of **Charity**.

News of Mother Teresa's selfless work spread around the world. She became famous and received many **awards**, including the Nobel Peace **Prize**. After she died, the Catholic Church made her a saint.

Think about the **difference** Mother Teresa made in the lives of others. What are some ways you could help someone in need feel cared for and loved?

Oh, the joys of those who are kind to the poor!
The LORD rescues them when they are in trouble.

PSALM 41:1 NLT

FIND THESE WORDS IN THE PUZZLE!

- ☐ TERESA
- ☐ INDIA
- ☐ POOR
- ☐ HUNGRY
- ☐ LONELY
- ☐ VOLUNTEER
- ☐ CHARITY
- ☐ AWARDS
- ☐ PRIZE
- ☐ DIFFERENCE

W	Y	T	I	R	A	H	C	V	L
V	A	R	B	B	V	G	O	L	T
F	S	L	M	V	W	L	R	O	N
T	E	D	H	H	U	M	R	N	E
F	R	C	R	N	U	K	P	E	Z
B	E	T	T	A	A	N	M	L	I
M	T	E	R	I	W	C	G	Y	R
X	E	F	D	Q	F	A	M	R	P
R	M	N	D	V	P	O	O	R	Y
D	I	F	F	E	R	E	N	C	E

Helen Keller

HELEN KELLER

A POWERFUL PRAYER

Helen Keller became **blind** and **deaf** as a little girl. It seemed impossible that she would be able to **learn** anything. But then a **teacher**, Anne Sullivan, helped Helen learn and live in the world around her.

God was always with Helen. She prayed and felt His power and love. With God's and Anne's help, Helen learned to read, write, and **speak**. Helen asked God for **power** to do more, and she accomplished great things. Helen gave speeches, **traveled** the world, met famous people, and received many **awards**.

Maybe there is something you want to do even better. Remember Helen's story. Ask God for power to do more.

I can do all things because Christ gives me the strength.

PHILIPPIANS 4:13

FIND THESE WORDS IN THE PUZZLE!

- ☐ HELEN
- ☐ BLIND
- ☐ DEAF
- ☐ LEARN
- ☐ TEACHER
- ☐ GOD
- ☐ SPEAK
- ☐ POWER
- ☐ TRAVELED
- ☐ AWARDS

V	T	R	Z	X	M	J	W	D	C
G	E	K	A	E	P	S	K	E	B
N	A	S	L	M	V	G	X	L	N
G	C	D	D	E	A	F	M	E	E
P	H	R	R	T	A	W	V	V	L
D	E	A	W	R	D	R	K	A	E
L	R	W	B	N	E	R	N	R	H
L	L	A	I	F	M	W	G	T	G
V	B	L	L	R	R	O	O	P	Z
L	B	T	C	D	D	H	R	P	Q

His tender mercy ... life has been my
divinest comfo... Him to dwell!
...er befall m... ...ell; For I kn...
... me, Jesu... ...e way my
...s each w... ...race for eve...
...ith the ... ...teps may f...
thirst m... ...re me, Lo...
I see; Gu... ...! A sprin...
3 All th... ...he fullness
...t rest to m... ...s house above
cloth... ...ealms of day
...gh endless ... This
...s ages Jesus led me all the way Jesus led me all th...

Fanny Crosby

FANNY CROSBY

SHE HAD JOY

Fanny Crosby couldn't see, but she would *not* allow **blindness** to make her **sad**. She had a positive **attitude** about life. She went to school in New York City and **learned** to read and write. Fanny had a **talent** for writing poems and Sunday school songs. In her lifetime, she wrote words for nearly nine thousand **songs**, always asking God to provide her with **ideas**.

Fanny's writing led her to become famous. She met leaders, like presidents and governors. She even read one of her **poems** in the United States Senate Chamber in Washington, DC.

Whenever you feel sorry for yourself, remember Fanny Crosby. Then put on a **smile** and a happy attitude.

A glad heart is good medicine,
but a broken spirit dries up the bones.
PROVERBS 17:22

FIND THESE WORDS IN THE PUZZLE!

- ☐ FANNY
- ☐ BLINDNESS
- ☐ SAD
- ☐ ATTITUDE
- ☐ LEARNED
- ☐ TALENT
- ☐ SONGS
- ☐ IDEAS
- ☐ POEMS
- ☐ SMILE

L	A	B	S	G	N	O	S	T	T
E	Q	T	B	R	P	W	A	Z	S
A	L	E	T	K	K	L	M	S	A
R	X	L	V	I	E	J	E	C	E
N	N	I	X	N	T	N	S	A	D
E	V	M	T	Y	D	U	Q	P	I
D	X	S	N	N	M	N	D	O	L
Q	M	V	I	N	V	R	Q	E	T
C	N	L	T	A	F	G	G	M	L
P	B	M	C	F	W	D	T	S	M

Gladys Aylward

GLADYS AYLWARD

SHE PRAYED

Gladys Aylward was a missionary who took care of more than a hundred **orphans** in China. This was a long time ago, when Japan and **China** were at war. Gladys needed to take the **children** someplace **safe** far away, so they started walking. They came to a **river** and couldn't cross, because the army had hidden all the boats.

"Let's ask God to **help** us," the children said. "He can do anything!"

Gladys and the children prayed, and God heard their **prayers**. A soldier showed up with **boats**. Then Gladys and the children **crossed** the river safely.

Remember, God will help you too. . .with whatever you need. Just ask, and He will hear your prayer.

Where will my help come from? My help comes from the Lord, Who made heaven and earth.

Psalm 121:1–2

FIND THESE WORDS IN THE PUZZLE!

- ☐ GLADYS
- ☐ ORPHANS
- ☐ CHINA
- ☐ CHILDREN
- ☐ SAFE
- ☐ RIVER
- ☐ HELP
- ☐ PRAYERS
- ☐ BOATS
- ☐ CROSSED

R	C	C	R	R	P	J	R	K	Q
S	M	H	C	H	I	N	A	M	J
A	C	M	I	P	L	E	H	R	T
F	R	P	S	L	B	C	I	G	S
E	O	R	Y	T	D	V	T	N	M
F	S	A	D	D	E	R	A	L	R
N	S	Y	A	R	N	H	E	X	R
W	E	E	L	M	P	M	F	N	N
L	D	R	G	R	D	L	M	K	T
L	D	S	O	W	B	O	A	T	S

ANSWER KEY

ANSWER KEY

AMY CARMICHAEL

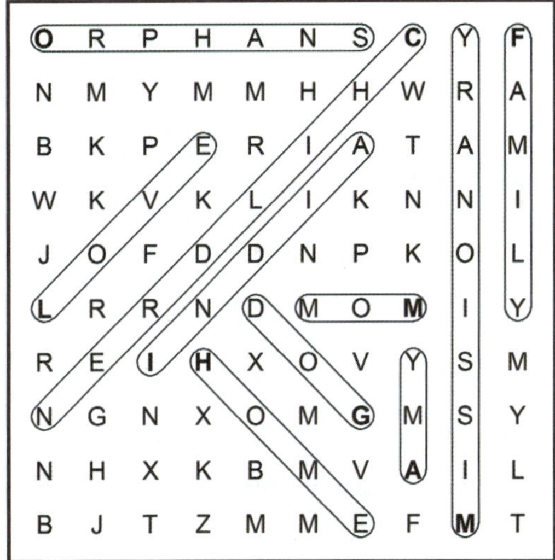

MAHALIA JACKSON

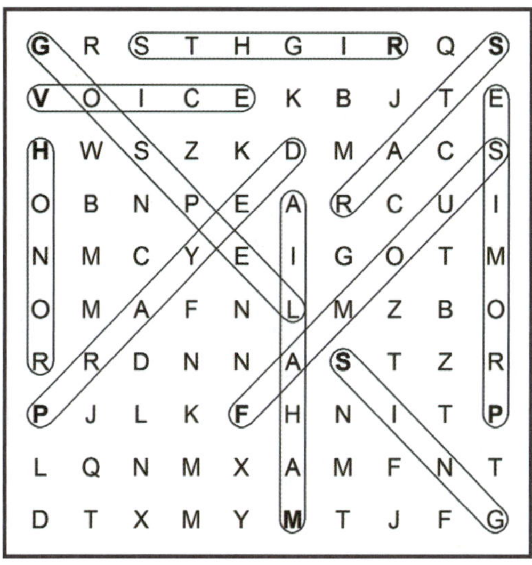

DEBORAH

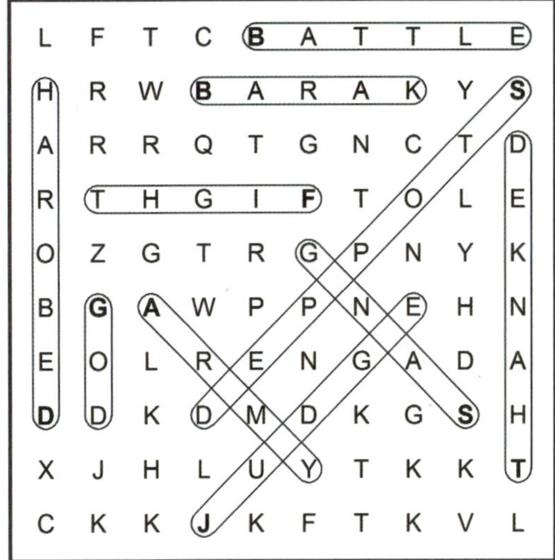

CORRIE TEN BOOM

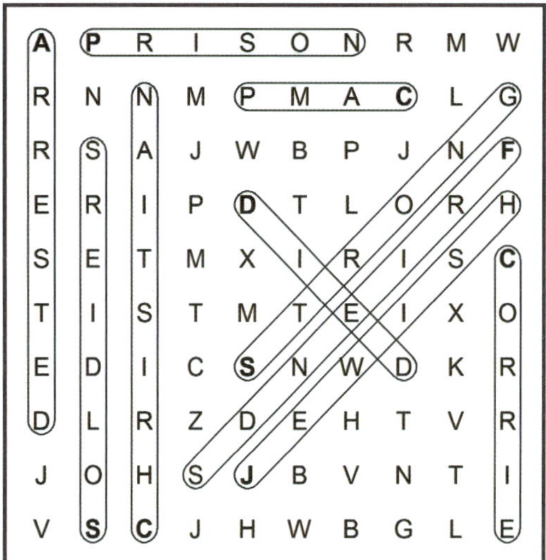

ANSWER KEY

HARRIET TUBMAN

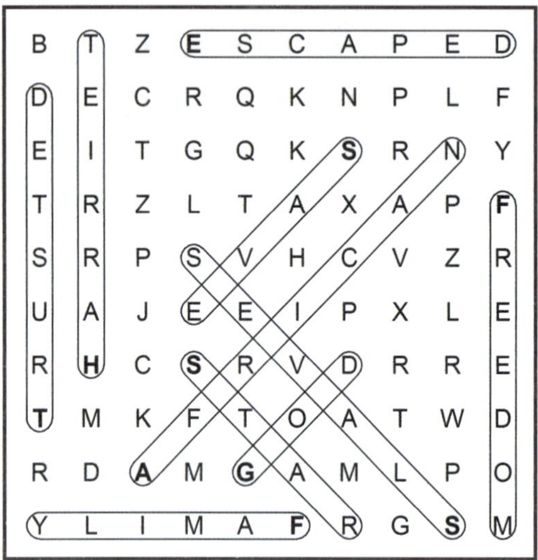

CATHERINE BOOTH

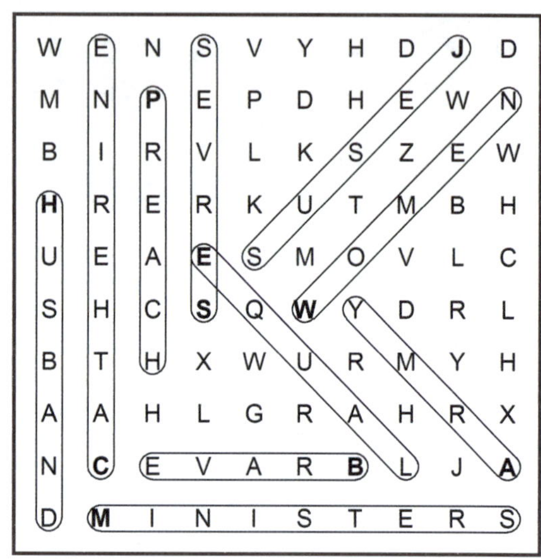

HANNAH

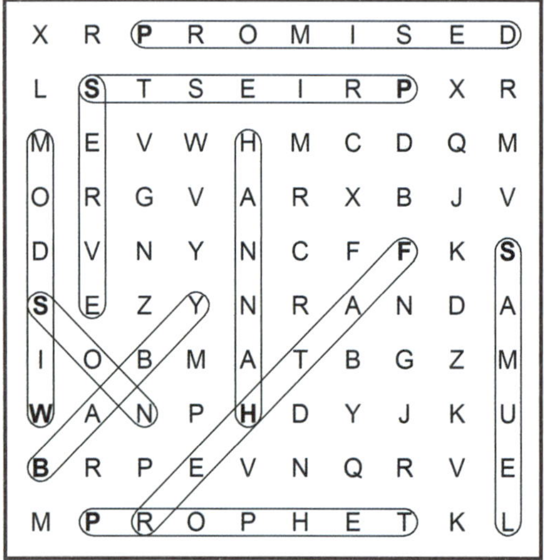

PANDITA RAMABAI

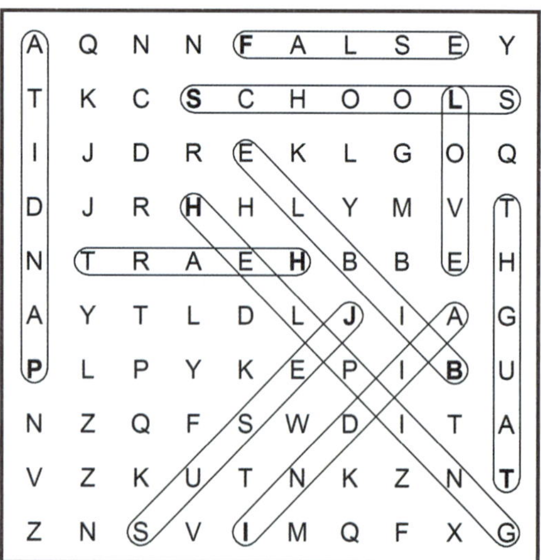

ANSWER KEY

FLORENCE NIGHTINGALE

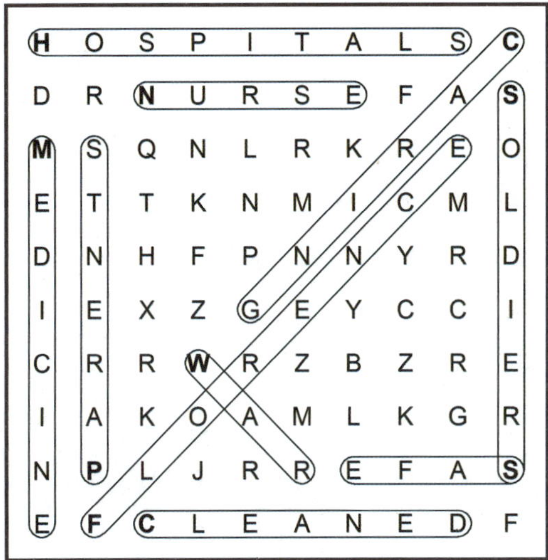

LOTTIE MOON

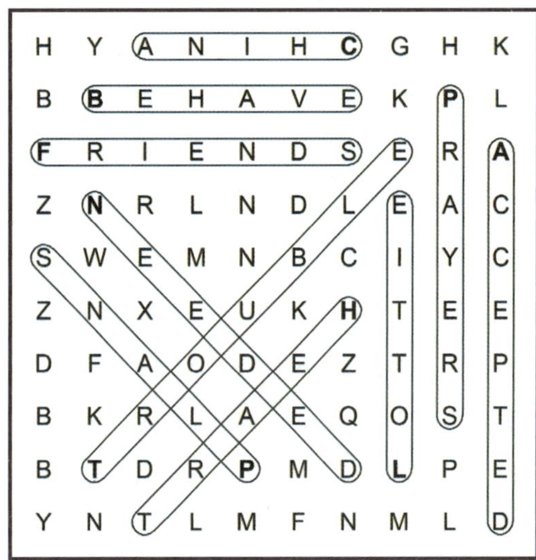

PHILLIS WHEATLEY

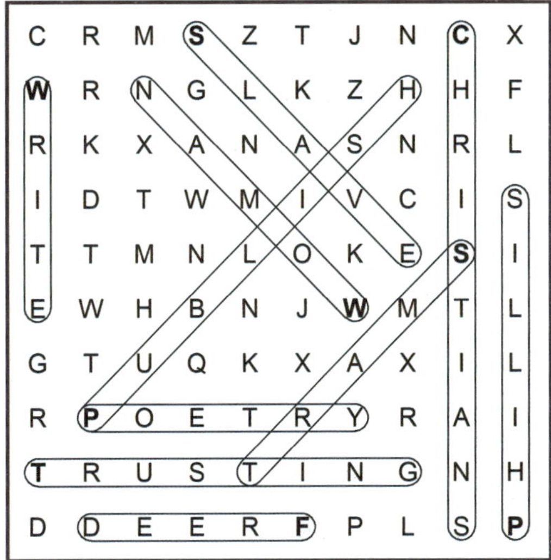

ESTHER

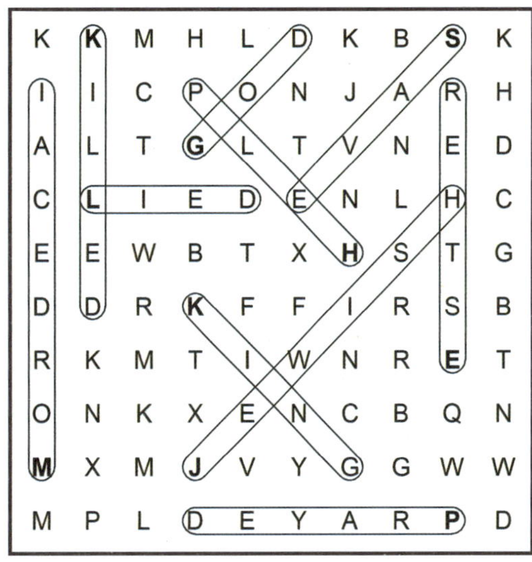

ANSWER KEY

FAYE EDGERTON

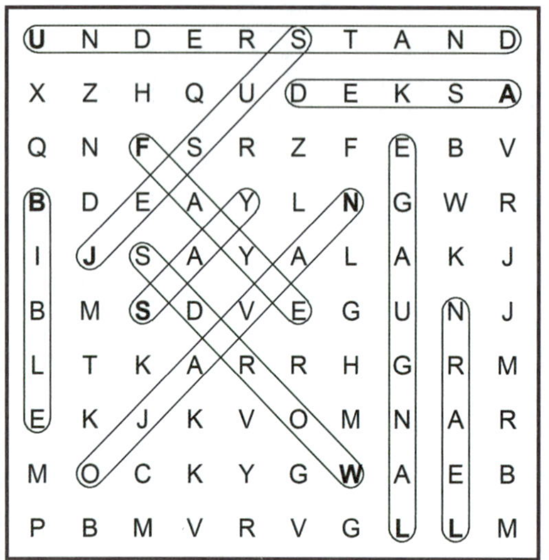

SOJOURNER TRUTH

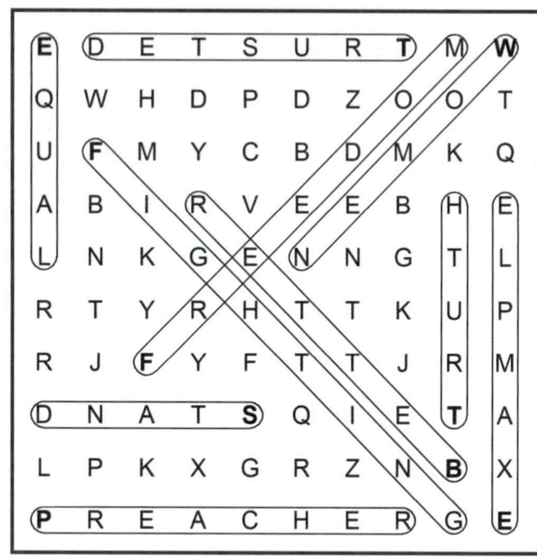

ELIZABETH FRY

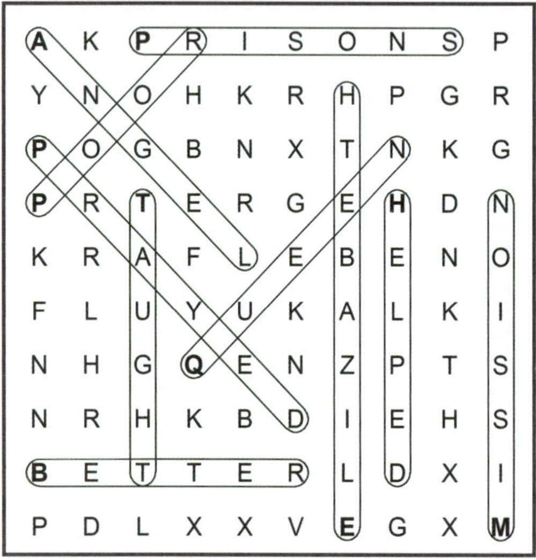

CLARA BARTON

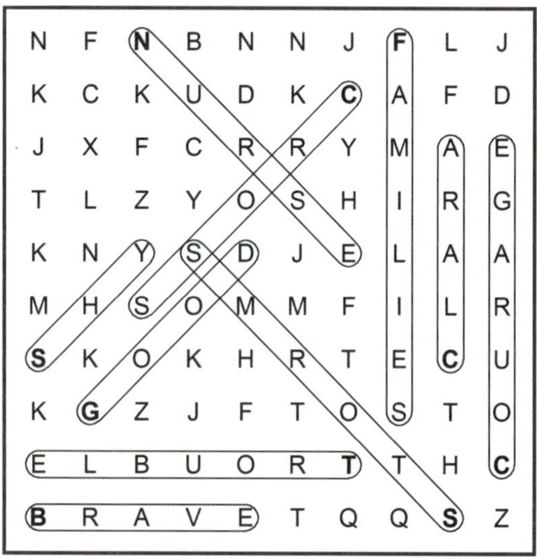

ANSWER KEY

EDITH SCHAEFFER

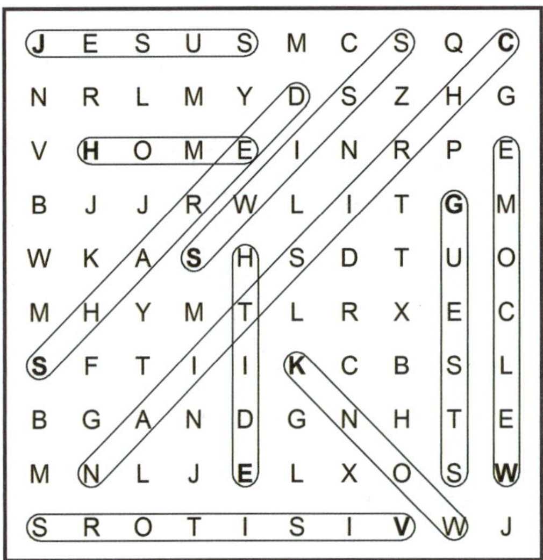

ESTHER IBANGA

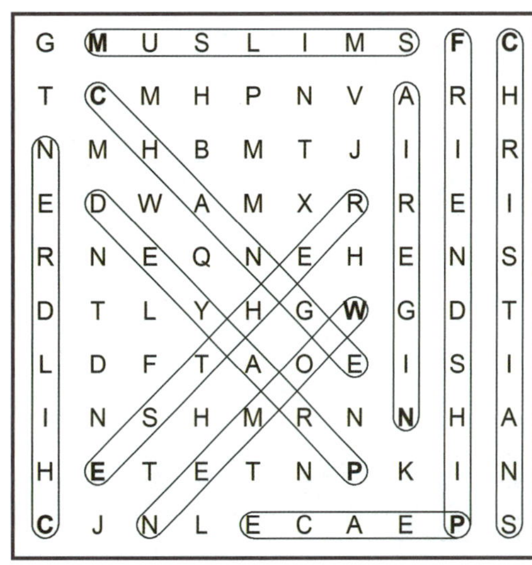

MARY SLESSOR

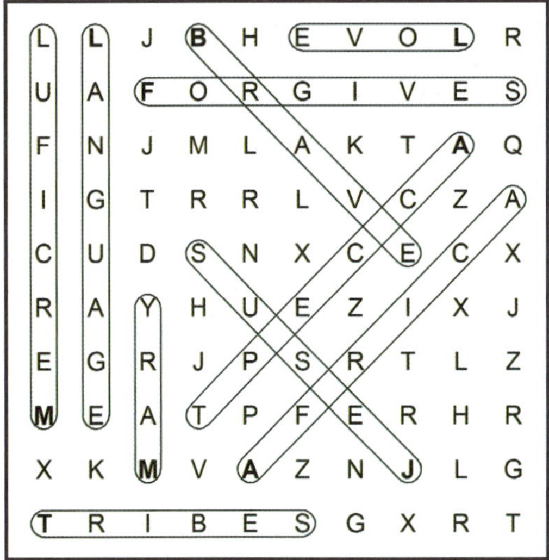

ANNE HUTCHINSON

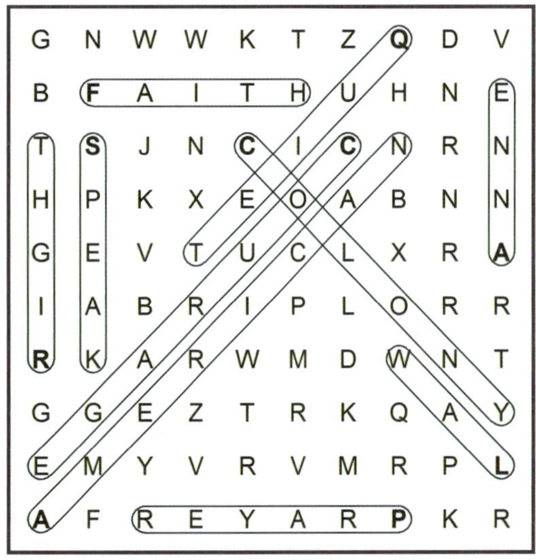

ANSWER KEY

MOTHER TERESA

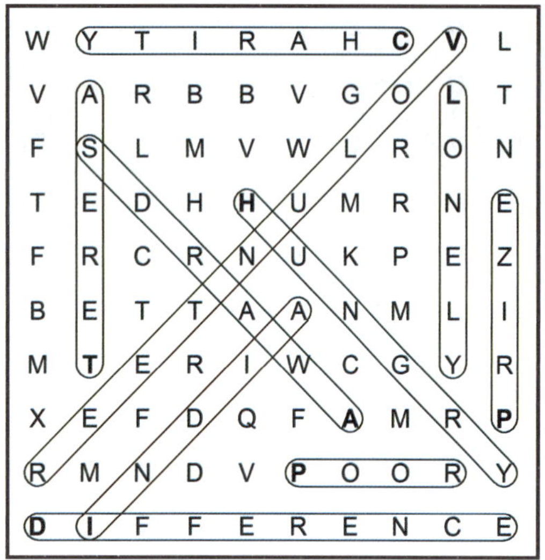

HELEN KELLER

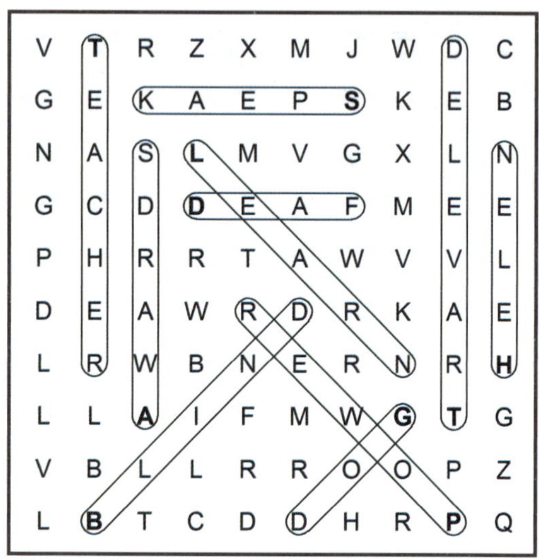

FANNY CROSBY

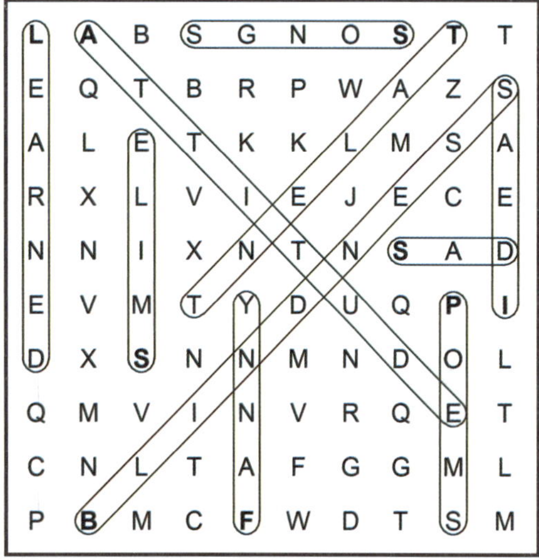

GLADYS AYLWARD

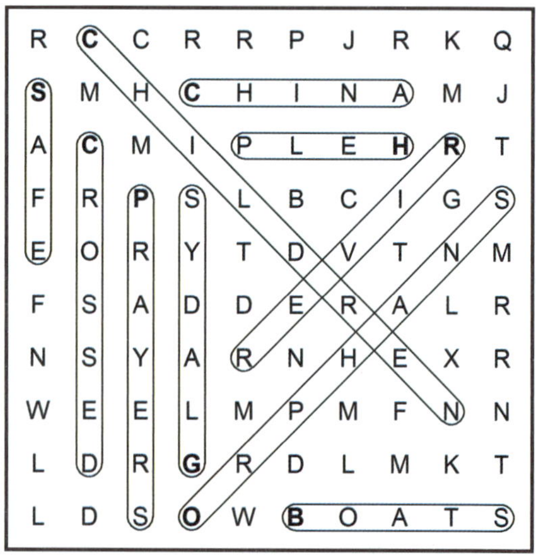

ALSO FOR COURAGEOUS GIRLS!

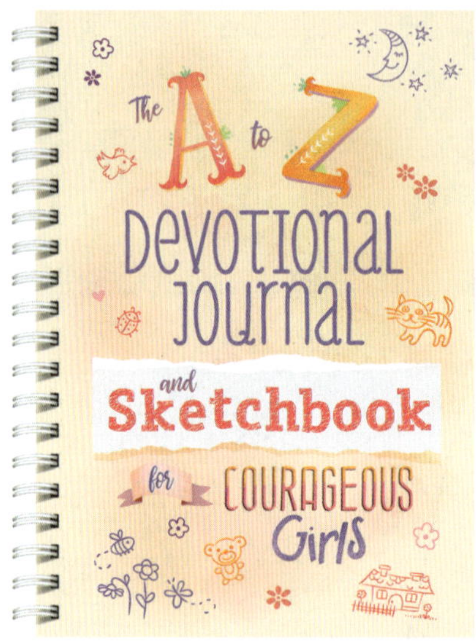

What makes a courageous girl of God? . . . Girls ages 5 and up will discover the answers in this delightful A to Z devotional journal and sketchbook! Each turn of the page introduces girls to a positive character trait for every letter of the alphabet alongside an inspiring devotional reading and related sketch and journal prompts.

Spiral bound / ISBN 978-1-63609-116-7